ANIMALOGY
ABOUT WILD ANIMALS

ILLUSTRATOR: IMMANUEL NICODEMUS

ENID MILTON

WORKBOOK PRESS LLC
187 E Warm Springs Rd,
Suite B285, Las Vegas, NV 89119, USA

Website: https://workbookpress.com/
Hotline: 1-888-818-4856
Email: admin@workbookpress.com

Ordering Information:
Quantity sales. Special discounts are available on quantity purchases by corporations, associations, and others.
For details, contact the publisher at the address above.

Library of Congress Control Number:
ISBN-13:   978-1-956017-37-3 (Paperback Version)

REV. DATE: 19/08/2021

ANIMALOGY

ABOUT WILD ANIMALS

TABLE OF CONTENTS

LEOPARD AND SPRINGBUCK

LEOPARD

Lurking patiently
Hungry
On to the springbuck's back he
Dropped.

SPRINGBUCK

Nibbling busily
Intent
On eating, not danger, so died.

PREDATOR AND PREY

LIONESS

Crouching in the grass
With muscles tensed
Watching, waiting,
Charged.

ZEBRA

Munching the grass
Watchful, wary
Of insidious sound,
Ran.

ZEBRA

Dragged down to the ground,
Struggling vainly
Relinquished his life,
Died.

LION

Gulping the meat
As if he'd starved,
And after the surfeit
Slept.

The Skunk

The skunk, whose habits we know well,
Produces a malodorous smell
Whenever he feels anxious fear
Of curious creatures coming near.

The stench offensive is so vile
You can detect it quite a while.
The skunk's defence is certainly
Effective for his privacy.

THE PORCUPINE

The porcupine plays dirty tricks
When you are not aware
Of his intention to cause pain.
Move nearer, if you dare!

That nasty brute will turn his back
And you will think that he
No longer cares what you can do.
But watch him, you will see.

The porcupine will quickly charge
In backward movement swift,
And those sharp quills will penetrate
Your skin and flesh - short shrift!

THAT GAPING MOUTH

The hippo has the biggest mouth
Which he will open wide
As if a dentist wants to see
The teeth that are inside.

Or maybe he wants to display
The tonsils in his throat.
But who would want to see such things?
They're not of any note.

But on the other hand it might
Be just a great big yawn.
Because he's tired and wants to sleep
Good manners he will scorn.

UGLY LITTLE WARTHOGS

A mother warthog runs around
With tail up straight and strong
Because her babies need to see
And follow her along.

Her body is so short and fat
She can't be seen among
The grass and plants which grow quite tall
And hide her from her young.

She's really quite an ugly beast
With warts below each eye
And long, flat snout she'll use to smell
And find her food supply.

She has two tusks which she can use
As tools to dig the ground
When she is hungry, and she knows
Where good food can be found.

She likes to sleep in earthy hole,
Her tusks are facing out
So enemies who dare disturb
Will suffer, there's no doubt.

SILLY BABOON

What are you doing, you silly baboon,
Sitting there in the middle of the road?
A car will bump you if you don't move soon.
Haven't you heard about the Highway Code?

Why can't you do something useful instead?
Or at least do something less dangerous.
Go join your cousins back there in the park,
But don't copy them and get boisterous.

They create such trouble in many ways.
We haven't found a way to deter them
From spreading the trash of tipped-over bins
And inspecting it all, every item.

We chased them away but they soon returned
To repeat their disgraceful behaviour.
The litter's still there, all over the place.
Our attempt to clean up was a failure.

You are the silliest creatures on earth,
And some people say that you look like us!
We think that's an insult, but we don't care.
It's too much trouble to make a big fuss.

THE FAT RHINOCEROS

I am a fat rhinoceros,
They say my shape's preposterous
But I don't care what others think, I'm happy as I am.
Perhaps I look quite comical
In senses anatomical,
With fat, round body, four short legs, you could think I'm a
sham.

My habits may seem ponderous,
Or sometimes even languorous,
But if you think I'm slow to move you make a big mistake.
My eyesight's poor, I don't see well,
But I run fast. I do excel
At fright'ning people when I charge, I really make them
quake.

My charge will sound quite thunderous
With pounding feet so vigorous,
But I intend to scare them so their irritations cease.
You'll think I'm just a surly brute
Without a single attribute
To make myself beloved by some - but all I want is peace.

DESERT SENTINELS

Sentinel guarding on top of a hill,
Tall lissome body is keeping quite still,
Small rounded ears are alert for a sound,
Bright little eyes always searching around.

Standing on hind legs with tail for support,
Front paws together with legs that look short,
Craning his neck to look out over grass,
Always on watch, hoping enemies pass.

Danger may come from all manner of things.
Eagle owls swoop down with wide outstretched wings,
Grabbing their prey with their talons so strong,
Back to their nests hauling Meerkat along.

Jackal approaching, so sound the alarm,
Make sure the little ones don't come to harm.
"Scuttle away, hide yourselves underground,
Go to a place where you cannot be found."

Promptly they run. A few seconds will pass.
Jackal sees nothing but dry tufts of grass.
He cannot get any Meerkat to eat,
He must continue his search for some meat.

The Crocodile's Teeth

Have you ever examined a mother croc's teeth
Spaced out in her very long jaw?
All the prey that she threatens would be petrified
With fear, if that's what they saw!

Did you know that a crocodile mother lays eggs
And carefully hides them away
In a hole in the ground? Then she covers them up
To keep all attackers at bay.

When the crocodile babies are ready to hatch
They start to break out of the shell,
Then they send out a cry which the mother croc hears
And rushes to make sure all's well.

Do you think you can guess how the mother croc moves
Her babies and eggs carefully?
In her mouth she will carry them to a safe pool
And watch that no predators see.

Do the babies get bitten by mother croc's teeth
When carried to safety that way?
No, of course not, she's careful and does them no harm.
She won't use her offspring for prey!

THE TREE THAT CATERS FOR MANY

The shy little dik-dik will creep out warily
And quickly get some food from his fav'rite tree.
The lowest level's his.

What does he eat?
The lowest leaves of the acacia tree.

The elegant impala walks with steps so light,
Goes to the tree to satisfy his appetite.
He knows he'll get his fill.

What does he eat?
The lower middle leaves of the acacia tree.

With hind legs, back and neck so vertical and straight
The gerenuk, while reaching up, will demonstrate
Just how he gets his meal.

What does he eat?
The upper middle leaves of the acacia tree.

The long-necked giraffe stretches up when he perceives
That his dark purple tongue can glean the luscious leaves.
The highest level's his.

What does he eat?
The top leaves of the acacia tree.

The elephant's trunk is not long enough that he
Can reach the food he craves, so he uproots the tree.
It topples to the ground.

Then what does he do?
He eats the top leaves of the acacia tree.

Hyenas are Horrible

They're ugly looking creatures with a dirty coloured skin.
Progressively as they grow old they get all mangy thin.
Their eerie howling in the night's a truly ghostly din.

They use their noses to smell out what creatures have passed by,
Then trot along the trails and paths with heads held very high.
They also watch for vultures which are circling in the sky.

The vultures hover at a place where predators have been.
They like to get their share of food before hyenas keen
Arrive to take the rest of it, and leave the gory scene.

Hyenas' jaws are strong; they crush the bones which others shun.
They eat the marrow from inside, that's what they've always done.
And that is only first course food, the feast has just begun.

They hunt at night when no-one sees the dirty tricks they play,
Like ganging up together to be sure of getting prey.
They'll even kill an injured beast which cannot run away.

These scavengers are cheeky things, they steal a lion's meat
By sneaking up and rushing in, then making quick retreat.
Whenever they can get the chance they'll practise this deceit.

Hyenas are horrible!

ELEPHANT'S TRUNK

An elephant's trunk is the strangest thing.
It looks like a very long nose.
He uses it in a medley of ways.
I'll tell you about some of those.

When elephant has a very big thirst
He'll suck up some water to drink,
Or if he is hot and needs to get cool
His trunk makes a shower in a wink.

I wonder how often his ears are washed
With water so cool; it depends
On whether he thinks it is much more fun
To squirt it all over his friends.

The end of his trunk has two sturdy lips
With which he can grasp all his food.
When many large mouthfuls of leaves go in
His mouth then his hunger's subdued.

An elephant's trunk has a sense of smell.
He lifts it to sniff at the air
To know what the weather will be today,
Or smell whether danger is near.

An elephant's trunk gives a soft caress
On bodies of those who have died.
A pachyderm's way of saying goodbye,
A gesture which seems dignified.

If elephant's trunk is just hanging down
He feels quite relaxed and secure.
He placidly stands or slowly plods on
Because there's no danger, he's sure.

But if the long trunk is up in the air
It means that his feelings are strong.
He's getting quite angry, you'd better go.
Departure you must not prolong.

LEOPARD AND CHEETAH LOOK ALIKE

A leopard and a cheetah look so very much the same.
If you're not sure just which is which then you should try and aim
To tell the differences, they're clear if you look carefully when
You see just one of them alone and stop to think again.

The leopard hunts at night: when all is dark he'll creep away
And climb a tree to wait there for the unsuspecting prey
To wander near, not knowing that death is his misfortune,
Because the leopard, springing down, will kill him off quite soon.

The cheetah, on the other hand, prefers the sun much more.
He'll watch and chase, run fast and catch, by stretching out a paw
To make his prey trip up and fall, so he can bite its throat
Thus killing it, then drag away, and time to eat devote.

The markings on their coats are not the same, so be awake.
The cheetah's spots are solid black. It's easy to mistake
For leopard's spots which are "rosettes", the centre part is white
And circled with a line of black; look carefully, get it right.

Their faces may seem similar, but look again, you'll find
That cheetah has two curvy lines that are quite well defined,
From eyes to lips, they look like tears that trickle down his face
As if he cries a lot, but no, that's really not the case.

THESE ANIMALS!

The biggest and the heaviest are elephants, I guess.
They say their weight increases to at least five tons, no less.
In spite of this great weight they can all swim when needs arise,
Though probably they'd all agree that swimming is unwise.

I do believe the cheetah is the fastest on the ground.
For movement swift and catching prey he's certainly renowned.
They say he's capable of speed of many miles an hour
And every leap that takes him on will show his muscle power.

Majestic is the word that's used of lion when he strolls
On open veld where he is seen approaching waterholes.
And when another creature dares to steal the meat he's left
He gives a loud resounding roar of anger at the theft.

The funny little warthogs are the ugliest I've seen.
The warts they have below their eyes just make them look so mean.
When adults run they always hold their tails up in the air.
They do it so the little ones can follow everywhere.

The sloth must be the laziest, his habits make you frown.
With long curved claws around a branch he hangs their upside down.
He is so lazy that he makes no effort to be clean,
His fur collects small insects and some algae which looks green.

The most repulsive creatures known must be hyenas foul.
They join together in a gang when they go on the prowl
To find some food, and often they attack an injured beast
Which cannot run - a dirty trick, to say the very least.

The gentle springbuck moves with grace as she looks round for food.
She nibbles grass, then lifts her head in watchful interlude.
Then when she's ready to eat more she steps so daintily
Towards the next lush mouthful there, still watching warily

The soft-skinned little dik-dik is the shyest of them all.
The greatest height he can achieve is fourteen inches tall.
And if by chance you see him there and startle him, he'll run
And then you'll know, without a doubt, the company he will shun.

Each animal is different as I'm sure you realise.
No doubt you'll think that some are good, and some you may despise.
Now you must make your own mind up, but first find out the facts,
For bad things can give wrong ideas, a good thing counteracts.